Listen to Light

Listen to Light

HAIKU

Raymond Roseliep

ALEMBIC PRESS · ITHACA, NEW YORK

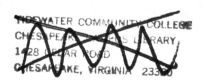

Most of the haiku and senryu in this book first appeared in the
following magazines: Bits, Blue Buildings, The Blue Canary, The
Blue Hotel, Bonsai, The Christian Century, Cicada (Canada), Delta
Epsilon Sigma Bulletin, Frogpond (Haiku Society of America),
Gusto, Haiku Journal, High/Coo, The Journal of Freshwater,
Leanfrog, Modern Haiku, Musepie, Outch (Japan and U.S.A.), The
Outlet (Loras College), Pilgrimage, Plainspeak, Poetry Nippon
(Japan), Portals, The Spoon River Quarterly, Studia Mystica,
Thoreau Journal Quarterly, Tweed (Australia), The Windless
Orchard, Yankee, and Yukuharu (Japan).

Library of Congress Cataloging in Publication Data

Roseliep, Raymond, 1917–
    Listen to light.

    I. Haiku, American.   I. Title.
PS3535.O675L54   811'.52   80-39854
ISBN 0-934184-05-4 (hardcover, library binding)
ISBN 0-934184-06-2 (paperback)

Publication of this book was made possible by a grant from the National Endowment for the Arts, a Federal agency.

The Foreword, "This Place, This Moment," was first published by the Academy of American Poets in *Poetry Pilot*.

"campfire extinguished" (page 62) won the Grand Prize, the Shugyo Takaha Award for 1980, from the Yuki Teikei Haiku Society of the United States and Canada.

"Mu" (page 85) in Japanese means "nothing; none; empty." In Zen, mu is the state of "mushin" (no-mind) wherein a person may experience enlightenment. The "Triptych" suggests the nothingness which is the everythingness of red when it becomes absorbed in itself. This oneness or unity is what people long before Eliot discovered to be "the still point of the turning world."

Sobi-Shi, who appears in a number of these poems, is the haigo or haiku name of the author.

The kanji or bamboo brush illustration of "light" on the cover and frontispiece and the kanji that precede the four sections of the book, illustrating the creatures named on the pages facing them, were drawn by Nobuo Hirasawa, of Tokyo, Japan. He also provided the signature of Sobi-Shi stamped on the cover of the hardbound edition.

for Elizabeth Searle Lamb

First Lady of Haiku

window
of sky
that's all

Foreword by the Author

This Place, This Moment

"Haiku is simply what is happening in this place, at this moment," declared Matsuo Basho, who is revered as the Shakespeare of haiku. Though this exquisite poetic structure originated almost 700 years ago in Japan, haiku began to flourish in the 17th century when Basho (b. 1644) adopted it as the vehicle for his enlightened perception of the universe and its details. Haiku realized a further dimensional flowering in the hands of three other masters, Yosa Buson (b.1715), Kobayashi Issa (b. 1763), and Masaoka Shiki (b. 1867). About a hundred years ago, English-speaking visitors to Japan discovered haiku; then Ezra Pound and the Imagists courted it in some of their writing explorations; and within the past twenty-five years great numbers of North Americans have taken to creating these miniature cameos.

Western adaptation of Japanese haiku is many-faceted and therefore elusive of strict definition. Since American and Canadian writers are still experimenting with the form as their adventurous classical masters had done and as contemporary Japanese poets are doing, a descriptive definition can be only a statement with qualifiers. Descriptively, then, haiku is a poem recording the essence of a moment keenly perceived, in which ideally physical nature is linked to human nature; usually untitled and unrhymed, it rarely consists of more than seventeen syllables, arranged most often in three lines, at times following a five, seven, and five syllable pattern. As Oriental haiku poets through the ages, our Western writers do not always distinguish between haiku and its off-spring senryu since the latter is really a satirical form of haiku, with greater stress on human events and the incongruities of things. "Haiku is the world as God made it," said eminent haiku historian R.H. Blyth, "senryu is the world as man sees it."

Flaubert's "fertile elements. . . seeking their form and awaiting their mold" are the stuff on which haiku are made. "There is no subject whatever," Basho believed, "that is not fit for haiku." Like this wandering unordained monk who lived by Zen, the most fortunate among Western haiku writers, in their penetration of the thingness of thing, the nowness of now, the hereness of here, and the suchness of such, will sometimes strike the invisible vein transporting the invisible current which is the deepest reality of all: the life-giving principle of material phenomena. If other Western haiku poets must settle for less, many of them do indeed manage to carve figures upon cherry-stones "so various, so beautiful, so new" that their creations intensify and exalt experience.

The most serious Western haiku poets keep as their touchstone old Basho's declaration of the haiku moment. They witness firsthand the real nature of things and sometimes even the Buddha nature of things. They aim to use a minimal number of words to report the instant of intuition, uniting the self and the object which has moved them emotionally. The very nature of art demands that they then share with others what Émile Zola called "a corner of Nature seen through a temperament." This discovery of some small astonishment in the animal, vegetable, and mineral world calls, in turn, for creative responsiveness. It is now up to the reader to enter into the original experience of the writer, to couple the beheld with the beholding, to identify with the "moment's monument," and to allow the captured enlightenment to lead wherever it will. As Auden and Valéry before him said of the poem, no haiku is ever finished, it is only abandoned. So the reader keeps getting on where the poet got off.

Firefly

快快
東

FIREFLY

the scheme
is
light

we
are all
in it

some
where
out there

opening spring
that bird
with the corkscrew voice

          spring peeper trio
     A, G sharp, B
               good enough for frogs

if frogs couldn't speak
you'd skip them
in grass

mockingbird:
what story
to tell

the look on the lark's face:
"I saw over cloud,
over over"

the wren
moves apart
from its song

```
                p!"
           u

         c
"Hic-
and your white undershorts
d
     i

        s

           a

              p

                 p

                    e

                       a

                          r   in pine

                                   what?bird
```

the woods boy
with the piccolo—
                         but isn't Blake dead?

PAN, WAKING

feel of earth,
flesh gleam,
foothold still dream

the old woman holds
lilac buds
to her good ear

                    violet
between   /   two toes
              detained

              stitching air
              ruby needle
              hummingbird

the hummingbird
motors wings
we miss

the black hen
eating outside
her shadow

homestead excavation
grandpa's jaw latching,
unlatching

heirloom rocker
rocking grandma
and older ghosts

in the tool shed
my father explaining
my 'growing tool'

on the boy's chest
a smudge of hair;
the bearded iris

lilyhold
on itself
before burst

ring of water
in a ring of ring
ringing water

the wet dream   the crescent moon

the Chinaman,
Santa María,
        bleached my blue jersey!

        Sistine Chapel:
        just above me the snug arc
        of a toenail

        brushing my sins
        the muscatel breath
        of the priest

the white iris
  I forgive
  myself

in the widow's veil
stars
blown from dandelion

                                    the bones of a bird
                              on the spring path of lovers
                                    not saying a word

holding your note,
bird in the bush
on my rice paper

for spring wind
plenty of room
in the kimono

be quiet inside
to hear the lotus open
its quivering bud

TEMPLE

before Buddha
the spider sits
suspended

.

with a rice cake
the child
with Buddha eyes

.

I leave my body;
the cricket too
off by itself

Ikon

i

my stone clots
under the ikon
    ruby of wounds

ii

side hole to Christ:
    my finger rage
    of ruby

iii

sun
    fracturing
        my ring

the firefly you caught
lights the church you make
with your hands

spider
and dollmaker
work side by side

the spider alone
recrosses the fine line
of being

spider midair:
I receive my self
returning

bathing you,
sick brother...
          the fallow field

ELEGY

he was the kid
who cut his vein
to pour in mine

Intimations of Immortality From Recollections of Early Sky Gazing

our
dust
part

for
star
part

must
part
us

—Sobi-Shi

the dark luck
Christ! of
tree seed

After Dusk

asleep
the firefly
  is fueling

sparks
however small
  light lovers

  our bodies
listen
  to light

Skylark

morning song
body salt and wood fern
on the tongue

you ask
if trees sing:
             hold me

your finger on
the climber rose...
blood runs uphill

our kiss
      emptying
            space

wind on the flesh,
what's left
of the moon

the gardener
hoeing peas:
his green sweat

sheep
cry best
in lavender dusk

monks chanting
the psalm tone
of the bee

I tried to bring you
that one cloud
in this cup of water

                    cloud
          the jet gives the unicorn
                a second horn

with peacock quill
she signs his gingko leaf
                        Marianne Moore

FLANNERY

the short night:
the peafowls'
long vowels...

Toward Evening

the vesper sparrow!
your breath weights
the small light

"One world
at a time,"
you nod past Thoreau,

kidney desk of foolscap,
the bird a comma
in the sky

for Katherine Anne Porter

light
lights a sky
Dante missed

POOL

lily
not touching me
nor I, it

no
one to touch
but breath

the hand
is mostly
water

also for KAP

heat wave:
tearing lettuce
for rain sound

even in the shade
a silver fire keeps flashing
from the soldier's blade

after *Tosca*
a mosquito
aria

putting Beethoven
back in its sleeve—
a fox barks

        peacock
looking in the lake
        fan all broken

                bald eagle
                downed.
                        wren song a nuisance

                        all day
                        the dove's red eye:
                        tonight the cat's

the barker cries;
the clown cries
crying

the clown glues a clown
in his scrapbook
of Picasso

on his crumpled bed
the clown huddles
into himself

hair in curlers,
she comes out to string
the morning-glory

bible ladies
passing the creek—
    our cow immersing

sea foam
reminding him
of something lost

buoy bell tinkle
beyond the sizzling
song of the deer mouse

pacing
the shore
the ship's cat

you're here
    the smell
    of water

minnow swish
of silver ass:
    we river rats

for Tom Reiter

formal garden:
6/8 and 2/4 time
of butterflies

in her formal garden
Sobi-Shi wears
his codpiece

the path
to and from the rose
is the same

asleep
bee and man
honeyworn

campfire extinguished,
the woman washing dishes
in a pan of stars

glaucoma:
rising
earlier

aware
of the heart:
handling glassware

glasses
lying on Basho
look on

setting
the egg timer
the wet nurse

for a whole minute
the steeplejack keeps trembling
in my soap bubble

he parts the drape
that sun flow in
her crewel forest

the white cane
comes out of dusk,
reënters it

"Old man" I whispered,
arms around my father:
no leaf moved

with his going
the birds go
nameless

dawn
at my fingers
    I join my body

skylark!
my clothes
fall upon me

Owl

autumn stillness:
the cracks
of your hand

leaves unleaf;
cicadas break
no promises

leaf over leaf
heaping upon them:
the old play checkers

wind lengthening
the pampas grass,
the baby's white hair

the blind man's
yellow pencil
in the rain

potato digging
she sings words
handed down

                          the hickory nut
                  out of its husk   in the hand
                          is itself again

            the space
            between the deer
            and the shot

wind in the eaves:
the hand spanking
breath into the child

dust storm;
gnarled hands powder
the newborn

after childbirth
she wants to see
the withered moor

the piping plover
mourns our being
on the dune

unknown weed
being
blue

once my friend. . .
spears
of dune grass

never expecting
the lilies in November
nor the small coffin

moonless wood
things only
as we see them

not seeing
things as they are,
seeing things as he is

in the lettuce core
the distant weeping
of a man

white orchid
on her coffin
        the pickle lady

cricket
mixed
with the mourners

the bat
upstaging
my disco cape

long after
the diesel horn
the horned owl

"Wiggins," I call
but my cat too
has found the full moon

on autumn wind
    my ancestors
and such wild birds

at my father's grave
the mourning dove
speaks soft German

my mother stock-still
before the balloon I put
on my father's grave

chainsong
of chain saw...
          the whippoorwill

continuous peel:
I re-create
my father's apple

eyes
listen for light
to crack

"Mu" Triptych:
              A Primary Color

dawn match
in cockscomb,
cry gone

        cardinal
        leaving
        my ruby

                pimiento
                on the fire engine
                        how now! Matisse

Love Song

I enter
your mirror

loving
you
in poor light

milkweed
fountain
flown

moth
nor lover's breath
disturb my candle

the figs hang loose:
the two of us
I said to Sobi-Shi

reading Issa
Sobi-Shi's
    fine cat

up the plum
not at all sure
Buson is not there

autumn river:
reeds walk
broken feet

music hall
quiet
cicada shell

Rheims in rain:
the tour guide
weeps softly

SEASCAPE

Auden is gone
gull
cry

sky
the surrounding
voice

carpet slippers
ferry
him

d. 29se73

THE BLUE CANARY

Equal parts
sky, picasso blood.
Shake well.

Chicago Picasso
the silence
around her

under
El Greco
the brown bag lunch

Snoopy
with Greek
mask

flowing
toward you
rivers meet

woods
word the night
in no known tongue

bird flight
tightening
mine

dawn
scraps
us

Crow

lost flake
            soul
is it you?

snow
first cancels
the white swan

the crow leaves
the black face
of the clock

                    snow things all still
                        rabbit breath
                                    carries

bowls of breath
shaping on the air:
soup line

she chops firewood
after his homily
on hell

but for "krohgogogok"
the snowy owl
is the white field

plum
thoughts
of
you
plumb
dark
in
the
snow

−Sobi-Shi

shoes wear out
your knoll
where the moon bloomed so

to bed
and trees overnight
where no tree ever grew

our song
in the piano stool.
day break

"I feel my child kick":
    on her head
    the jar of water

birthcry!
    the stars
    are all in place

the milkman
hums a homemade
moon song

the dressmaker
sings and sings,
mouth full of pins

light in her thimble
enters
the finger

WALT

musing
before a stove
of belly fire

the dark hand
offering Gandhi
carved in soap

cellist
finger on
the cheese slicer

the sailor
peeling potatoes
around himself

pausing
before the scrub water
to fix her hair

light
from an old dream
her bleached-out eyes

wringing out my socks
mother so wan
I wring my hands

on the night wind
I hear the silver pin
sing in your hip

day breaks
one perfect thing
itself

the pall bearers...
our Chinese goose
steps without looking

the cry
is here
where I buried it

ghost of my mother
on the clothesline waving:
flour sack dishtowel

i.v. dripping;
the chipping sparrow's
one pitch

after surgery
why a man dreams
he's had a child

bathing me
my nurse sings
"Jack-in-the-Pulpit"

                                        bathwater
                                    down the drain
                                        some of me

at the mouth
of the path
I took   once

more aware
than the bird
of its flight in wind

SCROOGE

nothing happens,
just falling snow
in the paperweight

TOAST

straw
sound of snow:
Wassail, Herr Handel!

MIDNIGHT CLEAR

bell
of cattle breath,
birth rope swinging

Christmas Eve:
butchers' knives
stop ringing

poet:
sackcloth
Santa

winter garden
   the white
  eggshells

          night walk:
          eyes
          of the hills

ordering my tombstone:
the cutter has me feel
his Gothic "R"

Sobi-Shi Writes His Epitaph

Six
foot
two:
six
foot
dark

Big
Dip-
per!

priest bread
whiteless
light

flake too quick
for a peephole
to the absolute

light
lights
light

About the Author

Father Raymond Roseliep was a member of the Department of English at Loras College in Dubuque, Iowa, for twenty years. Since his retirement from teaching in 1966 he has been resident chaplain at Holy Family Hall, an infirmary for Franciscan nuns in Dubuque.

Roseliep was a widely published and highly regarded master of traditional English verse forms when he began experimenting with haiku in 1960. This is the ninth collection of his haiku to appear since 1976. The major haiku periodicals, which include *Modern Haiku, Frogpond, High/Coo, Cicada* (Canada), *Outch* (Japan), and *Tweed* (Australia), publish Roseliep's haiku regularly and over seventy other magazines in various issues have printed his haiku, senryu, and haiku-stanza poems.

Roseliep has won both of the two annual haiku contests held in North America, the Harold G. Henderson Award from the Haiku Society of America in 1977 and the Shugyo Takaha Award (grand prize) from the Yuki Teikei Haiku Society of the United States and Canada in 1980.

Other Books by the Author

The Linen Bands (The Newman Press, 1961)
The Small Rain (The Newman Press, 1963)
Love Makes the Air Light (W.W. Norton
&. Company, Inc., 1965)
Voyages to the Inland Sea, IV. Essays and Poems.
Edited by John Judson. (University of
Wisconsin—La Crosse, 1974)
Flute Over Walden (Vagrom Chap Books, 1976)
Walk In Love (Juniper Press, 1976)
Light Footsteps (Juniper Press, 1976)
A Beautiful Woman Moves with Grace
(The Rook Press, 1976)
Sun in His Belly (High/Coo Press, 1977)
Step on the Rain (The Rook Press, 1977)
Wake to the Bell (The Rook Press, 1977)
A Day in the Life of Sobi-Shi (The Rook Press, 1978)
Sailing Bones (The Rook Press, 1978)
Sky in My Legs (Juniper Press, 1979)
Firefly in My Eyecup (High/Coo Press, 1979)
The Still Point (Uzzano Press, 1979)
A Roseliep Retrospective: Poems & Other Words By &
About Raymond Roseliep. Edited by David Dayton.
(Alembic Press, 1980)

Colophon

Raymond Roseliep designed this book in collaboration with David Dayton, who set the type in Goudy Old Style on a Compugraphic phototypesetter. The pages, which are Beckett eighty-pound offset stock, were printed by McNaughton & Gunn, Inc., of Ann Arbor, Michigan. Art Craft of Ithaca, Inc., printed the paperback cover and flyleaves and the hardcover jacket. Of the first edition of seven hundred fifty copies, five hundred were perfect-bound and two hundred fifty copies oversewn and bound into hard covers by Page Bindery, also of Ithaca, New York.